MW01273997

Pages Of My Soul

A Collection of Heart-Warming and Inspiring Works Of Poetry

Carol Baxter

CrossBooks™
A Division of LifeWay
1663 Liberty Drive
Bloomington, IN 47403
www.crossbooks.com
Phone: 1-866-879-0502

First published by CrossBooks 11/22/2011

ISBN: 978-1-4627-1157-4 (sc)

Printed in the United States of America

This book is printed on acid-free paper.

Any people depicted in stock imagery provided by Thinkstock are models, and such images are being used for illustrative purposes only.

Certain stock imagery © Thinkstock.

CROSSBOOKS
PUBLISHING

To my father who always believed in me,
family members and friends whose words
of encouragement kept me going.

Preface

Growing up in the Northwest, it was not hard to experience the beauty in Nature all around me. God's creation was always a wonder to me, even as a child. I remember playing in the woods and finding a little patch of moss with tiny pink flowers blossoming throughout. I was in awe.

Years went by and the wonderment got buried by the daily routines of life. I even turned my back on God for some time. Good thing He didn't turn His back on me. When my life turned upside down, there He was, picking me up, brushing me off and telling me to put one step in front of the other and find the tiny flowers with Him.

It took a while, but I started seeing the flowers again and knew I needed God in my life to raise my four children as a single mother. Not just raise my children, but raise them well, as independent, caring, responsible adults. As the years passed, there were tough times for sure, but my faith and my Christian friends kept me on the right path.

My path somehow was always connected with nature and the curiosities of life. One day while walking along a dry riverbank and looking at all the smooth rocks, a question arose: "Why are all the rocks so different? Why didn't God just make all rocks the same color and texture? I had taken geology classes in college, and I knew the answers science could tell me.. But that didn't matter. What mattered was what my heart, my God, was telling me: that we are all individuals, made special for a purpose, on purpose.

That was the beginning. I wrote my first poem, "It's just a rock". That was all it took, except my poems have gone deeper and more spiritual. Sometimes the words just pour onto the page. Those are the times I love writing the most; when I know it is a gift. It has to be a gift because I was not a very good writer in school and still can't spell to save me (spell check is my hero).

My poems have been described as "heartfelt," "emotional," "down-to-earth." I like that. I don't try to confuse the issue with a lot of hyperbole or hidden meaning. Some of my poems lend themselves well as greeting cards and the natural progression to photos came to be. To my surprise, my little camera caught some very good shots transforming my work into more than just a read, but more like a "coffee table book". A book that is not meant to be read cover to cover like a novel, but more to pick up, read a poem or two and ponder. I've been told I should include a box of tissues with my book; grown men have been known to cry while reading. So, fair warning, get out the tissue, sit back and let me share my poems with you.

The Soul Of Nature

It's Just A Rock

It's just a rock, a dirty stone,
With no heart, no voice, no thought of it's own.

It's just a rock, but on this beach,
No two alike, they're all unique.

It's just a rock, lying still on the ground,
Useless and lifeless, until I found.

This rock's a foundation, it's history is rare.
Each line, each color, it made me care.

That this rock's a part of life, like me.
Different from all others. So, I see,

It's just a rock and I'm just me.

Nature's Voice

While deep within the quiet surrounds
I burst inside with awe.
My every sense does overflow
From every breath I draw.

I love to be embraced by nature.
Embraced and taken in
To earth's own natural sanctuary
For quiet praise of Him.

How sad I am for those that walk
In nature and do not see.
That every twig or blade of grass
Holds peace and tranquility.

That even in the rain soaked wood
Nature is calling out.
To follow it's sweet love of life,
Stand still and let it shout.

Driftwood

Gathered driftwood from beach to shore
Those gnarled and beaten boughs.
Sanded smooth by wave and tide
For what my art allows.

I gathered driftwood from the sea
For what purpose some can't fathom.
Taken home to mark and score
Into something I imagine.

I love the burled and twisted limbs
And reveal each little quirk.
To embrace the beauty of His hand
And publish His great work.

So I gathered driftwood from the shore
To share my creations with you.
And pray Nature will inspire a human hand,
As artists are too few.

Mist Atop The Mountains

Mist atop the mountains,
plays gently with the scene.
Each quiet breathe of air,
reveals variations on the theme.

Sometimes flowing valleys
appear amid dewy haze.
Sometimes silent waterfalls
the distant hill displays.

Gazing cross the valley,
nature moves without a sound.
From mist atop the mountains,
tranquility here surrounds.

The Dandelion

Have you ever tried to rid the garden
Of those pesky yellow weeds?
Their roots are deeper than a well,
And they produce a million seeds.

The dandelion is a resilient plant
Much like my searching soul.
Strong roots that seek the fulfilling waters,
Of life's purpose and my goal.

So too, my search, like dandelions,
My questions are like seeds.
The more I know, the more I ask,
An unquenchable deep need.

I will never solve the riddles of life,
Like why He made that pesky weed.
But like it, I have a purpose too,
Grow deep roots and sew His seeds.

Raindrops Of Days

Days become as raindrops
And the weeks turn into streams.
Rivers are the changing years,
While life's ocean drowns my dreams.

My youth brought endless days
With visions as big as wonder.
Clouds were drifting images
And laughter sang like thunder.

Age has brought the rushing years
Lost are days on hidden ponds.
Times pass quick as lightning's flash
And suddenly my youth has gone.

How can I slow the passing
Of time that robs me of today?
How quickly life is moving
To that end that I must pay.

I'll savor the dew of every day
So life won't fall like rain.
I'll soak up the earth all around
Alas this gift won't be in vain.

Broken Paddle

Broken paddle, it's use well told,
The marks of faithful toil.
Dependable against the currents
And reassurance against the gale.

Taking me to sea and home,
I hold it's smooth wood tight.
Like security when most I fear
The approaching of the night.

Broken paddle, like broken dreams,
They served the purpose and more.
Without their beauty once when new
I'd loose sight of a possible shore.

Fall In The Northwest

A Northwest fall
Comes sudden overnight.
Evergreens scent the air
With their earthy delight.

A chilled wind gusts
And leaves release their hold
Rushing to the ground
Into a tapestry of gold.

Winds gust again
Fir trees bounce around
Needles fall as rain
Scattering music on the ground.

Sun filtered by clouds
Presenting spectacles of light
Beams streaming down
Giving heavenly insight

A Northwest Fall
Awakens all the senses
A place like none other.
This home that God blesses.

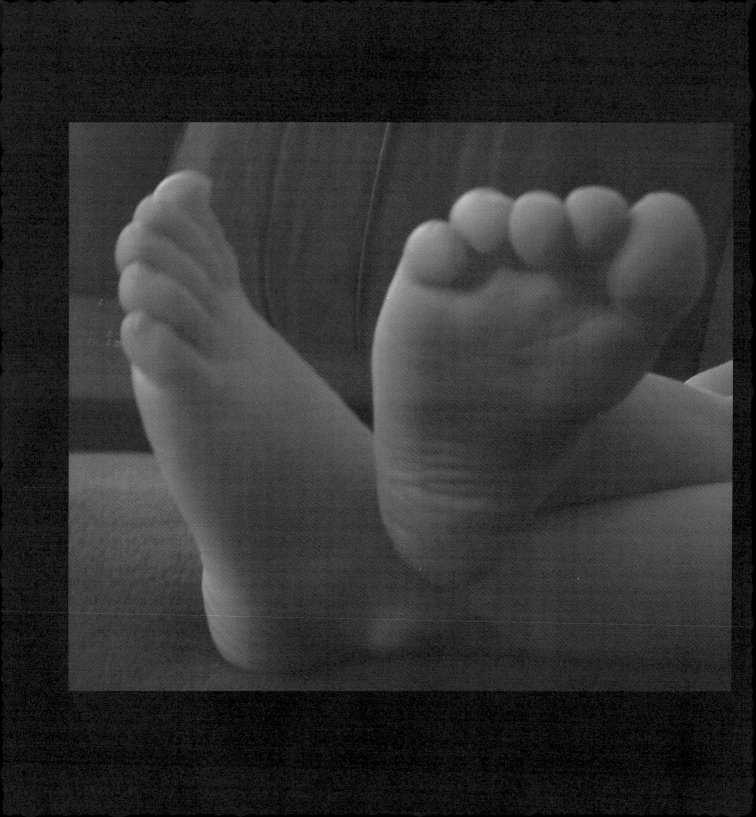

Tiny Souls

Sweet Baby's Face

Each stitch around made
With loving care.
Like God's creation,
This baby so fair.

Of perfect design
This tatted lace,
Like the features on
Sweet baby's face.

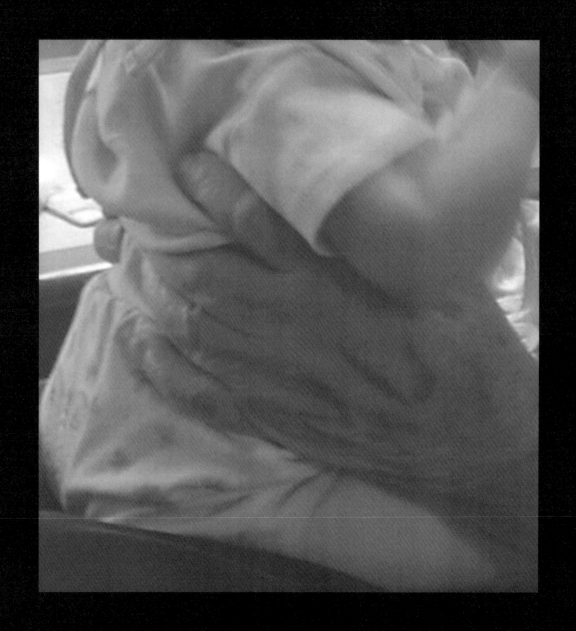

My Father's Hands

He went through the war,
And he fought with those hands,
To keep our country free.
He dug the rough soil
He tilled and he sowed
To feed a family of three.

His hands are so strong
You can see every line
Yet watch him hold my son.
Those same big hands
That same great grip
Has a gentleness all it's own.

His hands show our history
Our future now too.
So why those hands so mild?
They've worked so hard
And yet I know, it's because
He's holding onto my child.

My Bathtime

My bathtub's a magical bubbly place,
Where I don't even mind getting soap on my face.

I can play submarine or mermaid or whale,
And even pretend I'm a boat with a sail.

I can put suds on my belly button and between my toes,
And laugh when bubbles blow out of my nose.

I lather my hair till it stands up so high,
Then I make rabbit ears that reach to the sky.

With frogs on the curtain and ducks on the walls,
My bath tub's my favorite playroom of all.

And when I'm all done the best of that,
I get to cuddle up in a towel on your lap.

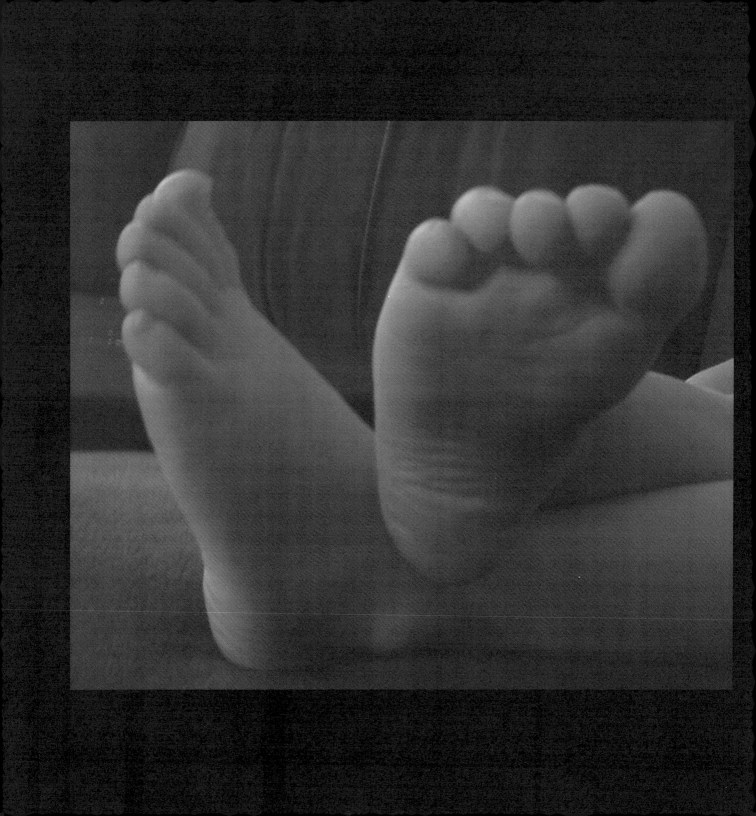

Babies In My Bed

Waking up in the dark
Alone in the night.
I bring them to bed
Secure from their fright.

I cuddle and sooth
Till they fall into sleep.
Soft breathe and wee sighs
Land soft on my cheek.

Their little toes twitch
And wake me a bit.
With a baby beside me
Sleeping is hard I admit.

But with each little sigh
And with each little jerk.
Minutes taken from slumber
I wouldn't trade for the earth.

The Soul Of Love

I Always Hope It's You

In solitude at end of day,
I am glad for thoughts a few.
Yet interrupted by phone's ring,
I always hope it's you.

Collecting mail from the day,
A bright envelope of blue.
Who has sent this caring card?
I always hope it's you.

Unexpected knock at the door
Is it someone that I know?
And as I near to open and see,
I always hope it's you.

Old couples hand in hand,
Love's depth in time just grew.
When I think ahead of my love,
I always hope it's you.

So with each call, each letter bright
Each moment that is true,
My greatest wish to share my life,
I always hope It's you.

Amazing Family

I can list a hundred families
Who have attained fortune and fame.
We try to imitate their lives,
And wish we held their name.

Families who were born to riches
Or made it good along the way.
Their money has bought them envy
With fans hovering as if prey.

But I know another family
That I would rather the world emulate.
Whose daily life's a struggle,
Most would never think to imitate.

.Grown children, they work together,
Each supporting the common bond.
A strong mother full of kindness,
She formed this unity and beyond

"I love you's" flow so freely
Yet each one is sincerely meant.
Gentle thoughts and words are heard,
Even in the most intense of argument.

An image of love, not wealth or fame,
Though they deserve it more than some
And the world would be better to imitate,
A family like this one.

Pools Of Love

What is love, this power unseen
That no one term defines?
Countless words express our heart
Yet different, they all combine.

Love is nothing physical
And hardly measured in the mind.
But nothing else we know
Can effect more of all mankind.

There is the love of country,
Of mother, father, sibling, child.
We show love for a pet or friend,
And even for songs compiled.

There is love for a passion,
And for the one love of our life.
Love for God and His Son.
Love between husband and wife.

A thousand songs are written
To express this one great need.
We will travel miles for it
Or resolve never again proceed.

Love's compared to rivers
To, puzzles, life's riddles and lies.
It's a shelter in the storm,
And the last words when someone dies.

One word cannot define
The many facets of love's whole.
Except perhaps an endless pool
Filled by waters from our soul.

Each droplet that is added
Whether love given or received
Is unique to our own love pool
And at home, never again to leave.

Love in a thousand many ways
Yet our pool will fill up never.
Because you see our hearts will grow
To a size we cannot measure.

It Takes A Fine Sailor

It takes a fine sailor to guide a ship to port.
It takes a loving wife with devotion and support.
It takes children to rely on when waves get rough.
It takes a safe harbor when weather calls his bluff.

Safe harbor where the sailor rests a weary head.
Safe harbor, caring people tending while he is in bed.
Safe feelings of comfort, right decisions, and health secure.
Safe knowing there are people dedicated to his cure.

Of Peaches And Of Sunsets

Of Peaches and of Sunsets,
What in common could there be?
Only variations of a hue,
At the most is all we see.

Did God design a marriage
T'ween fruit and a brilliant sky?
To show us ways of union
When two hearts unite and tie?

For it is the soft peach petal,
Like soft words t'ween two should stay.
Never crisp or with sarcasm,
But with understanding, not betray.

And the brilliance of a sunset,
Is like the joy that sparked the love,
That is meant for everlasting,
With blessings from God above.

But time forgets the passion.
As harsh suns will sear the peach.
So too bitter words will scorch
The heart and soul of each.

And the sunset's glow is hidden
When anger's cloud will come between.
Like lost dreams meet reality
And each day becomes routine.

Yet resilient is the peach tree.
Sunsets are hidden never replaced.
Like God's two perfect soul mates,
And love's vows can't be erased.

So too with both of you
Embracing pledges no one can sever.
Remembering the lessons taught,
Of Peaches and Sunsets forever.

Betrayed Love

Betrayal of Love is my greatest sadness.
It follows me into my dreams and becomes
A wound that I cannot seem to heal.
Love that was supposed to be, or promised
But never fulfilled and thrown away as if no one cared

I cared. My heart depended on it.
And my trust was eroded each time.
Love not just from a man, but mostly.
Also from a those special people I did not chose.
But who were to protect me from such hurts.

Cruel words and looks that start the betrayal.
With false interpretations of my intentions.
Misunderstanding my very being; my good heart.
Making me feel I am not who I thought.
And thereby causing me to doubt what I deserve.

These too, add to the dreams both day and night
That cause me deep sorrow for myself.
Betrayed time and time again creates the
Fraying of the fabric that is meant to hold together
A family and create an unbreakable bond.

And yet I forgive those that caused such pain.
Because they too suffered this lack and did not
Know how to break the cycle of shame and abject humility.
Humility that robs one of self respect, pride, dignity.
My heart grew to embrace them, love and care.

But too, there is betrayal of the bond of a man.
Not just one, but most of whom I cared.
Sometimes to other women, sometimes
To their own lusts and lack of true love.
But the hurt is the same, the dreams are the same.

Betrayal, oh how bitter the morning light sears
The feeling into my mind and causes me to feel less.
Why I ask, and ask again? Did I not love enough?
Why did I deserve to be left out of this special place?
The union of two people or that unconditional embrace.

And yet, God has given me, and I think all of us,
An inner strength that keeps us trusting in love.
Rising up from dark dreams and breaking through.
Making for a stronger self and more determined
Than ever to seek and give and teach true love.

Each day is renewed; even dreams fade away.
The rains wash some of the sadness of betrayal.
And so we can seek to share the sweetness of love.
Again, I pour out my love to those around. And I hope.
Because, without the hope of love, it won't be.

Thoughts In My Soul

Life Is Not Fair

When our lives lay in cinders
From the rages of the flames,
And we're scattered like cruel feathers
By fierce winds of hurricanes.
It's through lifted tears we sob
"Life is not fair" to those it claims.

That indiscriminate fate
That kiss of Mother Nature's wrath
Can't be fought or challenged
And so we receive our destined path.
We rebuild our shattered lives
Knowing "Life is not fair" have not or hath.

But what words do we then write,
When Nature is not holding the pen?
When "Life is not fair" is uttered
By those that steal thunder time, and time again?
It's called cruelty and greed
When life's fairness is dictated by men.

And unlike the strength begotten
By persevering through flood's unjust,
The man-made currents that drown us
Cause the rotting of our trust.
So, "Life's not fair" in nature,
But from man to man it's called "unjust".

What Do You Say

What do you say
When someone's beat the odds?
Who's looked into the face of cancer
And come out from its dark side.

What do you say
When someone truly lived?
In spite of pain and weakness,
As the holy ones in the Bible.

Who never cursed our Lord.
Who never blamed our Lord.
Who always held onto faith.
And praised the Lord always.

What do you say
When someone is so strong?
Who you know has suffered so much
And yet smiles and inspires.

You say thank you
You are a gift from God
You are His own, so I say
Thank you for being my hero.

Thoughts

Where do our thoughts go
When we finally leave this earth?
If not translated into verse
What are thoughts possibly worth?

If thoughts don't carry on
Why bother with thoughts at all?
Just wasted time and effort
While we pass from fall to fall.

But thoughts aren't a vacuum
Just ingesting those things acquired.
They're like a potter's hands
Creating from what's inspired.

The creation may be simple
Like bright smiles on sunny day.
Or the potter's clay may crack
When good thoughts stray far away.

So, is there an inner guardian,
Like a wall inside our mind?
Which thoughts become creations,
And which we dare not ever find.

Small, but mighty gaurdian
But with some awesome powers.
To fashion thoughts of goodness,
Or pot thoughts of poison flowers.

Thoughts becoming actions
That can enlighten many minds.
Or stir madness of a nation
To pose threats to all mankind.

Thoughts needn't be translated
Into verse or the written word.
When formed into our actions
Though they be silent, they are heard.

We personify our thinking,
Thoughts are not wasted after all.
Nurture that small guardian
So we protect others from the fall.

Don't bother where thoughts go
When we finally depart this realm.
If good we think and do
And love is always at the helm.

Our guardian will lead us
To act on thoughts to serve, not take.
And when our days are finished
Our thoughts will live by deeds we make.

Sadness Overcomes Me

Sadness overcomes me
And there is some comfort there.
A release from obligation
Of cheerfulness and care.

Energy sinks within me
As if pulled by a heavy weight.
And I ease into myself
Numb reprieve to my momentary fate.

Sadness overcomes me
And I let it take me to that place
Where nothing happy lives,
Where my grief can be embraced.

I need to feel the depth
That brief melancholy I have stole.
To give my joys rebirth,
After sadness overcomes my soul.

It Takes A Man

Some say that nothing changes
Man's nature is not taught.
And it's true we cannot force
A man to be what he is not.

But all men have within them
All parts of nature's ways.
And with direction for the growth
Can navigate the maze.

It takes inner determination
And a look at ones true self.
To see their own short comings
And put faults upon the shelf.

To take leaps for self improvement.
Opening up ones mind and heart.
And forgetting past behaviors
To take on life's better part.

These are the ways of true men,
Who walk, not stand in place.
For true men know the meaning
Of seeking God's truth and grace.

Few are those who chose to change
Most are stuck in their own ways.
But I know of one who took the trip
And knows the price it pays.

He's made mistakes along the way
His future not always bright.
But he kept the pace of progress
Of self betterment and right.

God sought him out so long ago
But he resisted with a fight.
Till broken and in great despair
He looked into the light.

Some men would just ignore this,
The meanings from above.
But this man has uncommon will
And accepted his God's love.

It's true that nothing changes
Unless you make it so.
Like only a few special men
Who are not afraid to grow.

Time To Grieve

Though their life's been good
And their path's been known
There is grief and sorrow still.

Though there are no regrets
For a life well spent
The parting is not our will.

Though tears can now flow
To help close the door
Warm memories the heart will fill.

The Reunion

At five years we unite
In excitement to meet
Those study hall comrades,
With shared secrets discrete.

We're exploring and young
With all options about.
The sky's still the limit
We still have no doubt.

Then through the years,
Some tough times and mistakes.
We show up less seldom
Fearing jeers and berates.

But there are still others who
Don't appear for the show.
Until they have climbed to
An impressive plateau.

Here I am, I'm a success,
Worth millions or more.
I'm above you, my classmates.
Look at me, envy and adore.

And what did it cost them
Friendships lost on the way?
To get to that pinnacle,
Prideful boasts on display.

To prove oneself worthy
To show off with pride.
Dismiss all the shortfalls
And dark secrets we hide.

How shallow our appearance
To wait till we prove
That we have a "Title"
We think we deserve.

But truth if be told
The only titles worth praise
Are titles for kindness,
And love through our days.

So, praise to those who appear
Grayed, balding and large
Just to see those old colleagues
For the souls that they are.

And reunite each year
Not to boast or proclaim
But to embrace true hearts
Of those without fame.

For The Love Of God

For the love of God I oft forget
To give thanks for my daily bread.
For the love of God I say not a word
In prayer when I lay my head.

For the love of God I forget I am blessed
To be born in this free place.
For the love of God I take for granted
His mercy and his grace.

For the love of God I need to stop,
stand silent in the night.
For the love of God raise my voice to Him,
Sing hallelujah with all my might .

Christmas Lights

Christmas lights delight our eyes,
And joyous songs bring smiles.
Gifts neath the tree await surprise,
And loved ones come from miles.

The symbols of our holiday,
We treasure and embrace.
We fill the stockings all the way,
And the lighted tree's in place.

But when all the shining lights go out,
When carols no longer chime,
When Christmas wrap is torn and gone,
It's Love, just love – that's Christmas time.

Please Find The Way

We cannot live forever,
But I know where I will be.
In the arms of my dear Savior
Unconditional love to me.

May I save a place for you?
In God's meadows we will stroll.
Then I'll never be without you,
And the beauty within your soul.

Please find the way to heaven
So we will never be apart.
And for all eternity
I will not suffer a broken heart.

Valentine Wish

This day's not just for sweethearts
Or souls that are entwined.
But for us to open up our hearts
For the love of all mankind.

The Perfect Valentine

On this day we seek our Valentine
To show love and dedication.
We want to shower them with gifts
And show signs of adoration.

But there is a special Valentine
Though often for granted taken.
Giving love that is unconditional
And commitment that's unshaken.

We won't get candies in heart box
Or champagne chilled and iced.
But the perfect Valentine to seek
Is our Savior Jesus Christ.

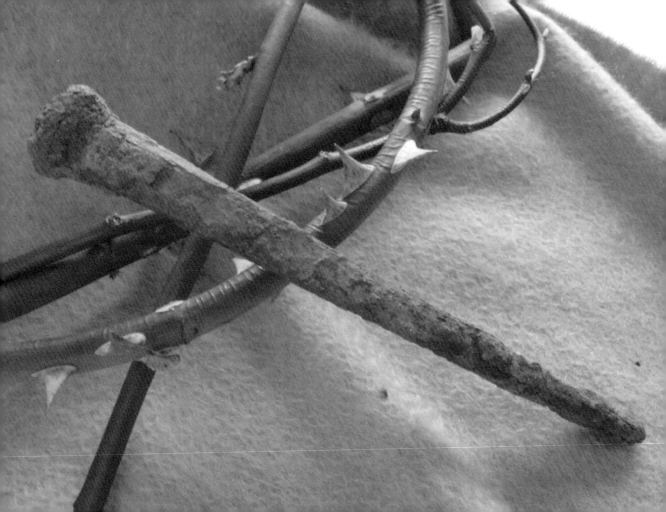

Wondrous Day

On this wondrous day we celebrate
Our Lord's assent to above.
He promised we would be with Him
Surrounded by His love.

But while we wait for that great day
He left us with a task,
That we should love and live our lives
As if it were our last.

Imagine each day Him sitting with us
Or walking by our side.
With each action and every word
Would we be His pride?

Or would our cold hearts be like salt
Poured onto His sweet blood.
And his suffering on our behalf
Give insult to Him above.

We know the walk to follow Him
He showed us all the way.
He taught us to seek God, not man
For drink and bread each day.

His greatest prayer for us left behind
We'd seek the truth with lust.
But maybe our true prayer should be
Mankind would see Him in us.

Walking With Jesus

I must have died that night,
For I was walking with the Lord.
Gentle peace filled our midst
And new life in me was pourd.

His love was overwhelming,
Acceptance beyond all measure.
That when I woke that day
I wanted to fall back asleep forever.

I don't recall of what we spoke,
But He knew me and new my name.
I dwelled in unconditional love
And felt freed from every shame.

I used to have a fear of death,
That daunting vast unknown.
But after that walk with My Lord
I look forward to His home.

Maybe Christmas

Our lives are so very busy
Work and family fill our days.
Weeks evaporate like water
And passing months become a haze.

I'll call that friend tomorrow
I've too much to do today.
Mom will understand
If I don't phone her, she'll be ok.

But at Christmas time we're called
To send out thoughtful cards.
We'll visit distant relatives
Or telephone with kind regards.

We plan a day together
At church to sing in candle light.
And remember why our Savior
Was born that humble, perfect night.

It's at Christmas time
We take a breath, and priorities are clear.
So maybe we should try
To have Christmas more times each year.

The Soul Of My Family

To My Children

Spread my ash
Neath a flowering tree,
So with the bloom
My smile you'll see.

And when the wind
Rustles through the leaf
You'll hear my words
For peace, calm and relief.

Let strong branch
Support child at play
Like my strength
Supported you each day.

When shade you seek
From harshest sun.
Remember my love
Still protects each one.

Year's new growth,
As with your family,
Will blossom your hearts
Like the flowering tree.

If You Could Hear Me Mom

May you now be without worry,
May your brow be unfurled.
May you be joyful and silly,
May your smile be uncurled.

May you finally shout and sing out loud,
May you be filled with glee.
May you slide down rainbows,
May you not be so afraid.

May your sprit find peace,
May your mind ease from strain.
May you relax from tensions,
May you release the grip of pain.

May you see mercy and goodness,
May you know your Lord.
May you be surrounded with love,
May your eternity He hold.

The Greatest Fisherman

Do you remember when I was eight
We sat silent in that old boat?
I found the worms we used for bait
And you tied a cork for a float.

And when you felt a fish on your line
You handed that pole to me.
Pretending all along it was mine
My pride of the catch to be.

I can't recall you ever catching a fish,
Though try and try as you may.
But Dad, you have the greatest catch,
My pride and love each day.

Step Mother

What daunting role a Mother's task,
But the Step Mother's role more tasking.
For Mother love from babe's first breath
While for Steps it's for the asking.

You come into a family's past,
No knowledge of what children shared.
Yet embrace them in collective sole
As if all their life you have cared.

It must be hard to embrace the role
Of Step Mother to ones not your own.
But yet, I know of no other Mom
I 'd share my Daughters and my Sons.

He Was Skipper Of Many Ships

He was skipper of many ships
And he mastered them all well.
With firm hand on helm and sail,
He navigated thru storm and swell.

His direction was from a compass
That pointed out right from wrong.
It pointed to integrity, honor trust,
And a purpose my whole life long.

Home was his safe harbor
Filled with humor love and respect.
He whistled and sang while working,
A feeling of security I could expect.

He could make just about anything .
Just give him the right tool.
His workshop was a tidy ship
And safety was his rule.

Skipper to the young and old
Trusting a job to be done as taught.
Shaping lives through self confidence
But no penalty if done not.

Though firm a skipper was my dad,
He had a very tender spot,
For children and for babies,
He could not resist a little tot.

He had to hold a baby,
And he walked them till asleep.
Then lay them down so tenderly
They never made a peep.

This fondness passed to me and mine,
I see this tenderness each day.
Learned from this skipper with a heart
Loving children was his way.

A lifetime skipper at one post
His humility served him best
Sailing the jagged rocks of layoffs
Put his compass to the test.

And when the winds blew in dark clouds
Of disappointment and great loss,
He remained the skipper of the ship
Hoisted sails and took it safe across.

He knew the storms would pass in time,
Showing what life is all about.
There is safety in the passageway,
Stay on a true and narrow route.

I've lost the skipper of my ship,
But though we are now apart,
I know his compass stays with me,
You see, he's the Captain of my heart.

I Watched My Mother Die Today

I watched my mother die today.
And although not unexpected,
Her final breath ripped at my heart
As if we were connected.

Sudden grief overwhelmed my being,
I felt I could not breathe.
Overflowing tears became a river
As I watched her pass and leave.

Her parting sounds were not of peace,
But I know not from her soul.
Her spirit had already gone,
And her body not in control.

My mother's soul left with my kiss,
And my promise to remember,
Each lesson taught, the right, the wrong
With glowing love, like embers.

I watched my mother die today,
But I know she will live forever.
In hearts eternally blessed and touched
And love even death can't sever.

A very special poem written for my birthday, by my son, Ryan Riddock

Mom

The best part of me is you

On good days, eggs bendict hits the spot
On good days, it's easy to meet new people
On good days, being creative comes naturally
On good days, the sun, rain, wind, and snow all make me smile

On bad days, there's always tomorrow
On bad days, eggs benedict still hits the spot
On bad days, being alone is spiritual healing
On bad days, wine is mental healing

Everyday I smile
Everyday I try to be helpful to others
Everyday I take time to enjoy the simple things
Everyday I love my family with all my heart

All these things I do
You do too
So, the best part of me
Is you

Your son,
Ryan

Inspirations

The following people provided special inspiration for particular poems. Their souls gave me additional insight into the many ways people touch one another and I thank them dearly for being part of my life.

Amazing Family – Inspired by my dear friends the Dickinsons.
Of Peaches and Of Sunsets – Written for the wedding of my daughter, Darcie to Gabe.
What Do You Say – Inspired by a co-worker with breast cancer, Gail.
It Takes A Man – Inspired by my good friend, Trey Shelton.
Time To Grieve – Inspired by my children's Great Auntie Betty.
Step Mother – Inspired by my children's wonderful Step Mother, Pat.

Special Inspirations come from my extraordinary children and their families who show love, kindness, humor, and dignity as part of their daily lives.

CPSIA information can be obtained
at www.ICGtesting.com
Printed in the USA
LVIW020554120313
323773LV00001BA